The Cedar Plank Mask

AN ACTIVITY BOOK ages 9-12
by Nan McNutt

Design and illustration by
Yasu Osawa

Westcoast Art by
Greg Colfax and George David

ISBN 1-57061-117-3

©1997 Nan McNutt & Associates

SASQUATCH BOOKS
SEATTLE

We dedicate this book to
Maria David
and in loving memory of
Lloyd Colfax

Our special thanks to
Greig Arnold, Bill Holm, and
Jeannette Mills for their time,
knowledge and commitment;
to The Petersburg Writers
for their readings;
and to Tarry Lindquist and her
5th grade class for making sure
this book is for kids.

Note for parents and teachers:

While the actual cover of this book can
be used for the main cut-and-paste
activity, we have also included an extra
full-color "cover insert" for the child's
use, bound into the middle of the book
to preserve the book's cover.

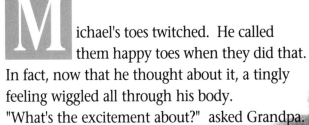ichael's toes twitched. He called them happy toes when they did that. In fact, now that he thought about it, a tingly feeling wiggled all through his body.
"What's the excitement about?" asked Grandpa.

It seemed to Michael that Grandpa could feel just about everything he felt.
"We're going to the museum today, Grandpa, and I bet we'll see some real Indian masks."
Michael leaned toward his Grandpa, his voice almost a whisper.
"Maybe, we'll even see one that great, great Grandpa made."
Grandpa grinned, "Well, maybe so."

At the museum Michael's class met Wilson, their guide.
"He looks like me," thought Michael. "He must be Indian too."
Wilson showed the students where to hang their coats and led them into an exhibit room full of masks.
"Have a seat," said Wilson as he sat down on the floor. Michael sat down next to his friend John.
"If you were to begin carving this Mask," said Wilson, holding up the mask of a man-like being, "what shape would you want the block of wood to be?"
Maria raised her hand first.
"Maybe, a sort of triangular shape."
Wilson held up a block of wood.
"Something like this? A prism?" he added. Everyone in the class nodded, "Yes, a prism."

Wilson continued, "Different groups of Indian people use various shapes when beginning to carve a mask. What other shapes might be good for carving masks?" As the students suggested shapes, Wilson passed around blocks of wood, prisms, half spheres, rectangles and squares.

Then Wilson held up a flat board. "We use planks split from a cedar log to make masks, too." Everyone looked puzzled. "While you explore the museum on your own," said Wilson, "look for the masks made from split cedar planks."

irst, Michael and John looked at the huge bird masks with white eye sockets, black beaks, red mouths and red flaring nostrils.
"Fearsome looking, huh!" whispered John.
"Yeah! And look how big these masks are," said Michael.
"I never thought masks could be so big."
Wilson joined them.
"These masks are worn by the Kwakiutl people. They are so huge that a mask must be tied to the dancer's body."
Wilson continued.
"When a dancer wants to snap the bird's beak he pulls a cord with one hand or his mouth.
"The beak snaps!" exclaimed Michael and John.

ext Michael and John met
Maria at the exhibit case
filled with face masks. The Tlingit,
Haida, and Tsimshian people who
carved these made the masks look
like real people. Some masks had
wrinkles, some had hair, some looked
spooky, and some even looked like
clowns.
"I bet these masks were made from half
circles," said Maria.
Wilson nodded, "You students are so
quick." Then he added, "but, now I'm
going to show you something else."
"I know," John was beaming,
"I bet it's the masks made from cedar
planks."

5

They joined other students already at the display of cedar plank masks. Wolves glared with huge eyes and sharp teeth. Ravens and Thunderbirds peered past curved beaks. Loops and scrolls decorated the top of other masks called Lightning Serpents.
"These masks are also called headdresses, because they are worn above the eyes of the dancer," explained Wilson.

"They were made by Indians who live on the western tip of Washington State, the Makah, and the west coast of Vancouver Island, the Nuu-chah-nulth." Then Wilson smiled and added, "I'm from a Nuu-chah-nulth group, the Ditidaht. What about you, Michael?"
"I am Makah!" Michael said proudly.

While the students looked at the cedar plank masks, Wilson handed out paper models of brightly colored plank masks. Excitedly everyone cut and assembled masks. They studied the display case to see if their mask looked like any of the real masks. "Why aren't there any masks that looked exactly like our paper masks?" asked Michael.

"That's because there should never be two masks that look exactly alike," said Wilson.

"Each mask is special and is passed down in a family from one generation to the next."

"Does every Indian family have a mask?" asked Michael.

"No, I'm afraid not," said Wilson. "During the late 1800's and early 1900's our people were told to abandon their traditional ways. Few masks were made or danced then."

Wilson added, "But new ones are being made today. Next time you come I'll show you some masks I have made and danced."

Michael thought about masks all the way home on the bus. He could hardly wait to tell Grandpa about them. "Grandpa!" he yelled as he swung the front door open. "Grandpa, guess what I saw at the museum?" Michael gasped for air. Grandpa just smiled. He had a pretty good idea from the paper mask in Michael's hand.

"Saw the real thing, huh?" said Grandpa.

"Oh, Grandpa, it was the best! Those old people really knew how to make great masks."

Grandpa nodded. "They really knew what they were doing. They knew about a lot of things." Then Grandpa turned toward his bedroom beckoning Michael to follow.

In the corner of Grandpa's bedroom sat several old trunks hidden by piles of blankets. Grandpa stooped over one of the trunks. "Haven't opened this in a long time, Michael, but I think we better do it now." Michael's eyes widened. He had never noticed the rusty trunks before. Grandpa pulled out a bundle of dark blue cloth. Michael saw something large inside. His stomach began to flutter.

"It's been a long time since I've danced with this," Grandpa's voice was low, "long before you were born."

Slowly and delicately he unfolded the blue cloth. Michael could see the shape of wooden scrolls which crowned the head, and then the bold eyes.

Grandpa held up the Lightning Serpent Mask. Michael could hardly breathe.

"This mask was given to me by your great grandfather, to use and to pass on." Grandpa straightened his back, pulling himself up tall. "It's time, Michael, that you learn about our traditions." Grandpa paused as he placed the mask on Michael's head.

Michael looked down.

A stillness came over him.

Grandpa continued. "There's a lot of work to do and much to learn, but I know you're ready to take care of our family's mask."

Raven Design

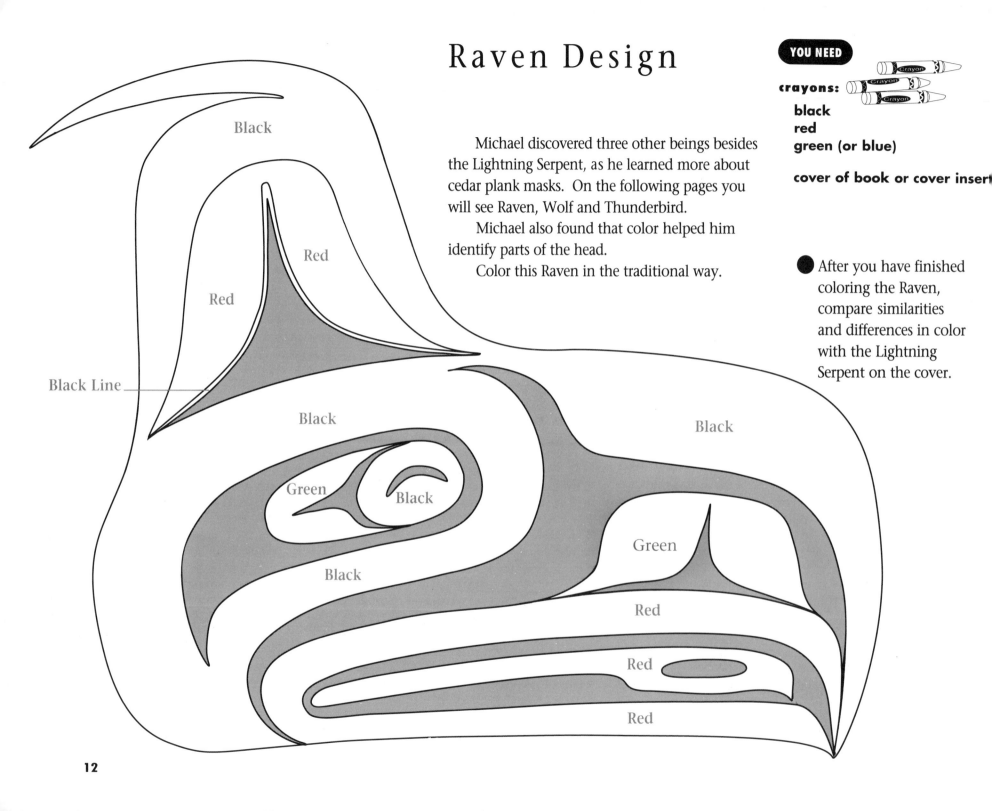

Black

Red

Red

Black Line

Black

Black

Green

Black

Black

Red

Red

Red

Green

YOU NEED

crayons:
black
red
green (or blue)

cover of book or cover insert

Michael discovered three other beings besides the Lightning Serpent, as he learned more about cedar plank masks. On the following pages you will see Raven, Wolf and Thunderbird.

Michael also found that color helped him identify parts of the head.

Color this Raven in the traditional way.

After you have finished coloring the Raven, compare similarities and differences in color with the Lightning Serpent on the cover.

Head Parts of Wolf

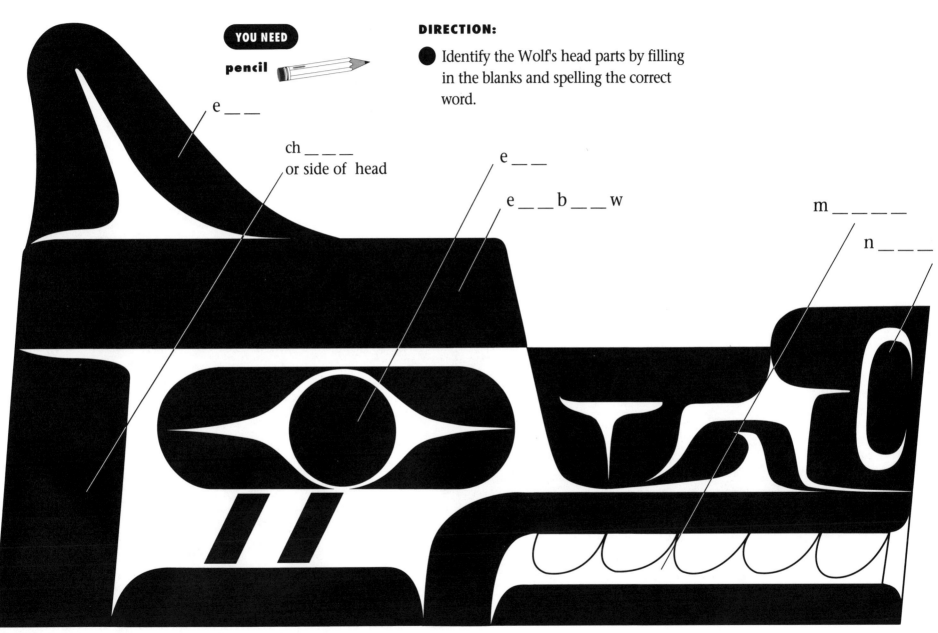

YOU NEED

pencil

DIRECTION:

● Identify the Wolf's head parts by filling in the blanks and spelling the correct word.

e _ _

ch _ _ _
or side of head

e _ _

e _ _ b _ _ w

m _ _ _ _ _

n _ _ _ _

Wolf Puzzle #1

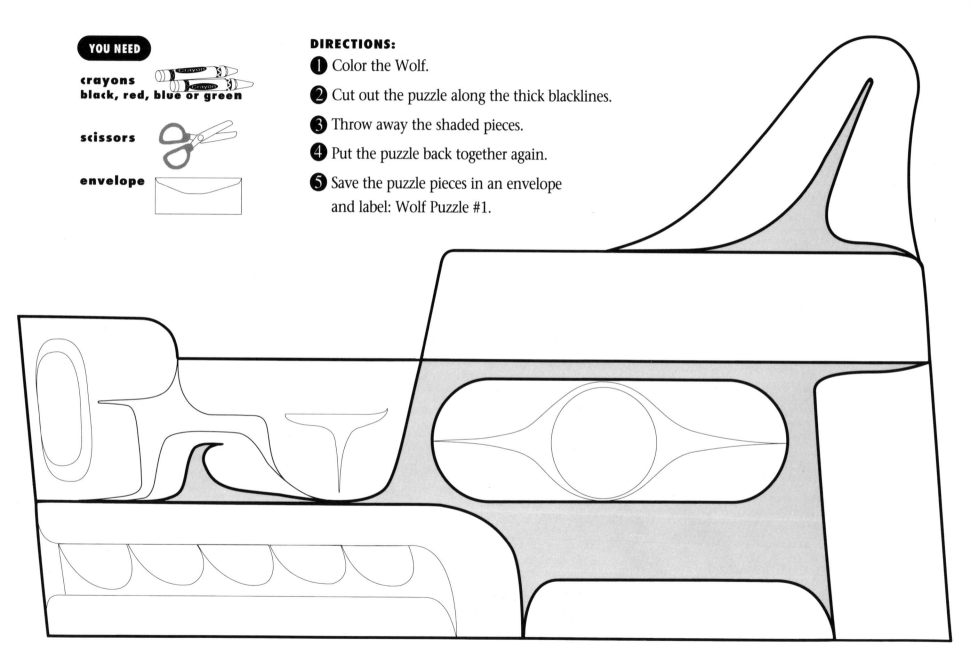

YOU NEED

crayons
black, red, blue or green

scissors

envelope

DIRECTIONS:

1 Color the Wolf.

2 Cut out the puzzle along the thick blacklines.

3 Throw away the shaded pieces.

4 Put the puzzle back together again.

5 Save the puzzle pieces in an envelope
and label: Wolf Puzzle #1.

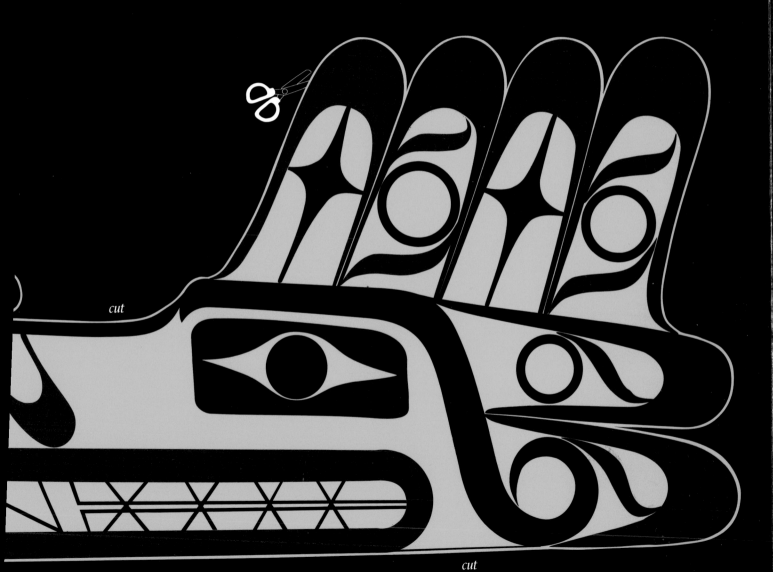

cut

cut

cut

cut

Fur or Feathers?

● Fill in the blanks and spell the correct word to identify the Wolf's head parts.

YOU NEED

pencil

Your best guess!

_____

e _ _

e _ _ b _ _ w

e _ _

ch _ _ _ _
or side of
head

n _ _ _ _

m _ _ _ _ _

Answers:

ear, eyebrow, eye, nose, mouth, cheek   these could be correct. Only the artist really knows.

What was your best guess, extension of the ear, feathers, fur, decoration? All of

Wolf Puzzle #2

YOU NEED

black, red, blue or green crayons

scissors

envelope

DIRECTIONS

1. Color the Wolf.
2. Cut it out along the thick black lines.
3. Throw away the shaded pieces.
4. Put the puzzle together.
5. Save the pieces in a envelope #2.

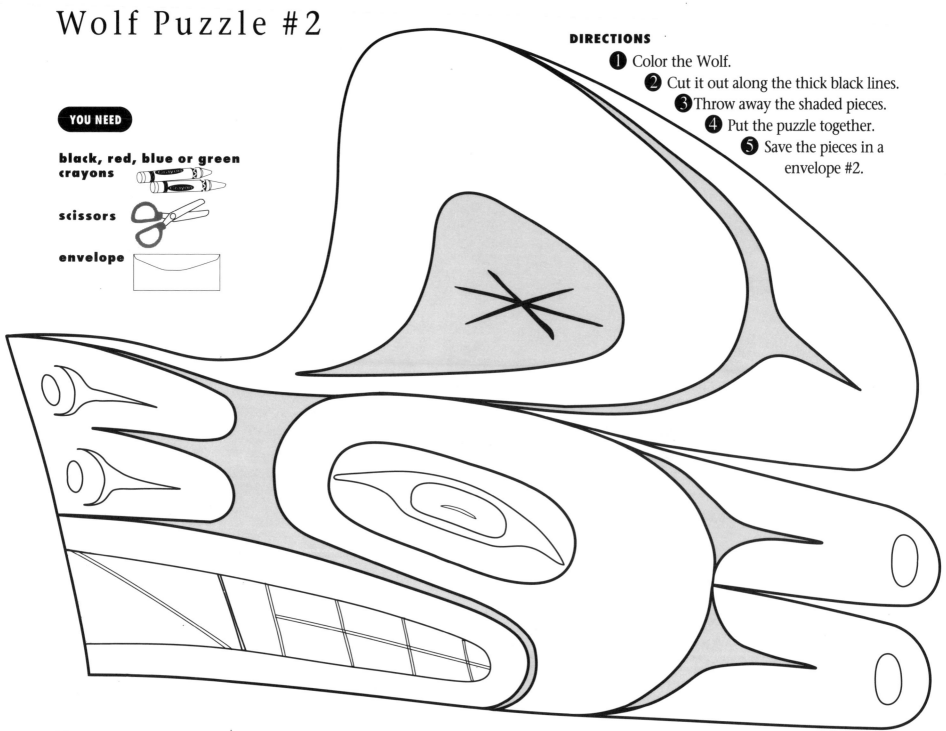

Design your own Wolf!

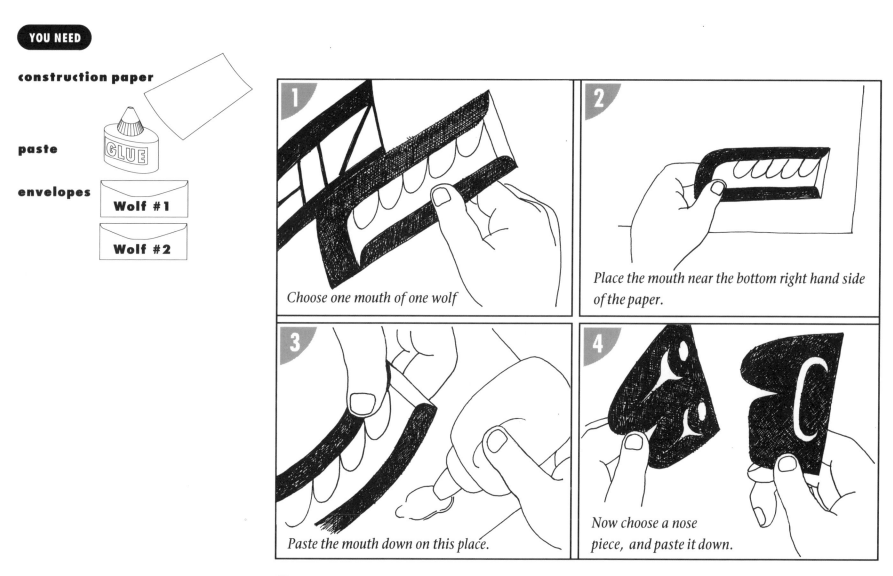

1 Choose one mouth of one wolf

2 Place the mouth near the bottom right hand side of the paper.

3 Paste the mouth down on this place.

4 Now choose a nose piece, and paste it down.

● Continue selecting, and pasting all the parts.

17

Head parts from "U"

Many head parts on cedar plank masks are made with a "U" form. Finish drawing these "U" forms and guess what head part they might be.

YOU NEED

pencil

The "U" has a secret rule.
Here is a poem to help you discover it.

No matter what "U" look like

U're a useful tool !

One bulky body

Two pointy legs,

It's a simple rule.

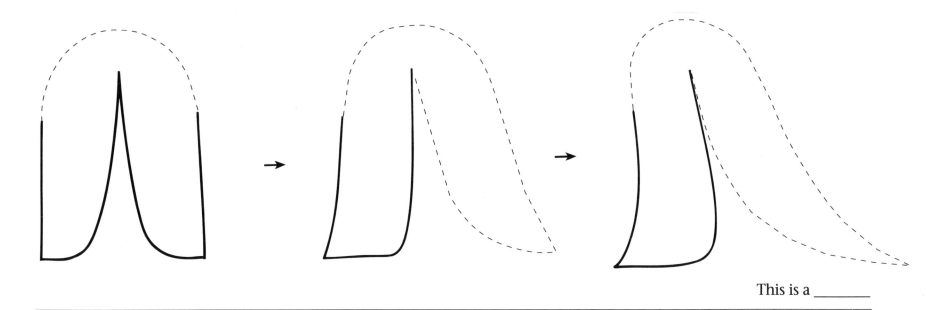

This is a _____

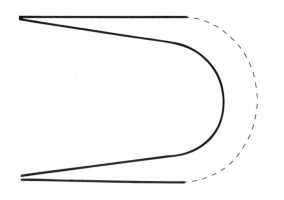 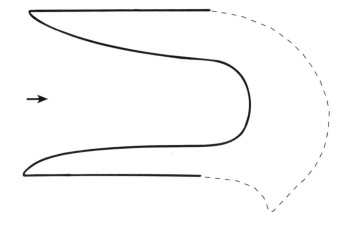 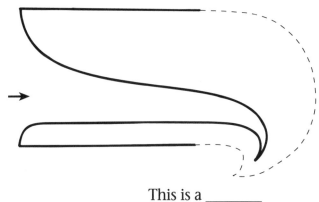

This is a _____

18

Answer: ear beak

Special Designs

Can you group these designs?

YOU NEED

Crayons

● Color the **Dashes** black.

● Color the **Stars** blue.

● Color the **Curlicues** Red.

Hint: There are three each.
Now locate each on one of
the masks in this book.

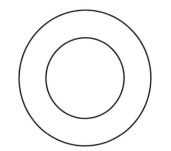

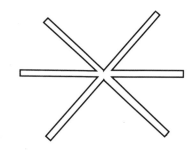

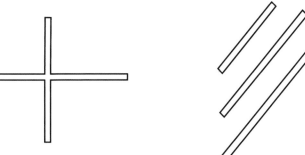

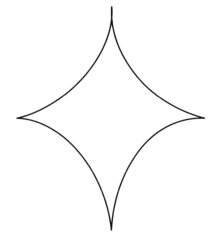

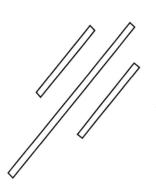

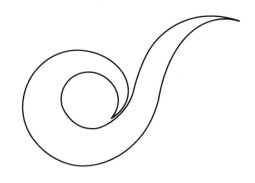

Answer:

Curlicues   Dashes   Stars

19

Thunderbirds
by two artists

These two Thunderbirds represent the styles of two different artists, George David and Greg Colfax.

● Can you describe the artists' styles? Look at the both Thunderbirds and compare them.

YOU NEED

pencil

George David's style:

_____

_____

_____

_____

_____

George David

20

Can you identify the artists' other drawings
in this book?

George David / page(s) _____
Greg Colfax / page(s) _____

Greg Colfax's style:

_____
_____
_____

Greg Colfax

Answer:
Greg Colfax: Pages 13 and 14
George David: Cover, pages 12 , 15 and 16

Make a Mask

thick paper 8 1/2"x 11"

scissors

pencil

black marker

tape

stapler

DIRECTIONS:

- Choose one Thunderbird that you like.
- Place the thick paper next to the Thunderbird you have chosen.

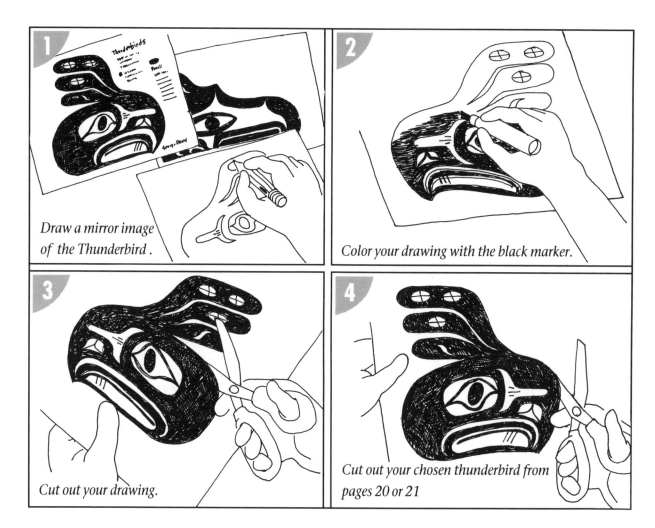

1 Draw a mirror image of the Thunderbird.

2 Color your drawing with the black marker.

3 Cut out your drawing.

4 Cut out your chosen thunderbird from pages 20 or 21

22

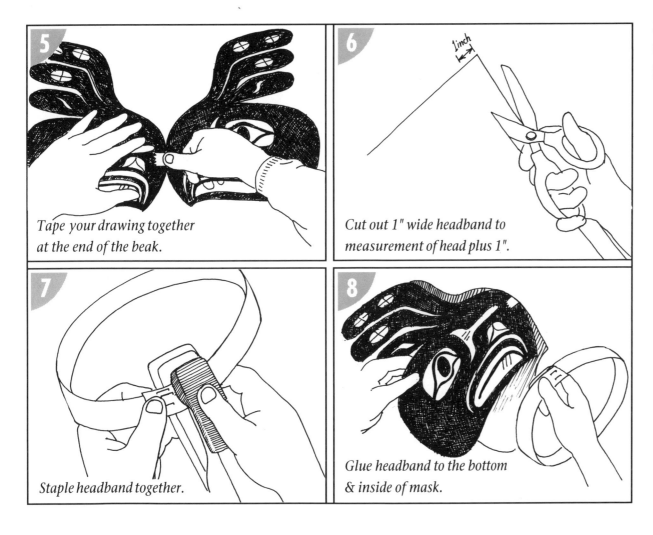

5 Tape your drawing together at the end of the beak.

6 Cut out 1" wide headband to measurement of head plus 1".

1 inch

7 Staple headband together.

8 Glue headband to the bottom & inside of mask.

Mask is worn just above the eyes and on the forehead of the dancer.

Lightning Serpent Mask

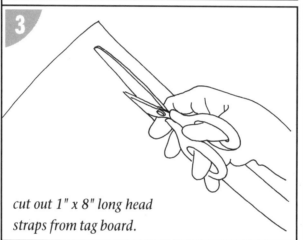

1. Cut out two sides of mask.

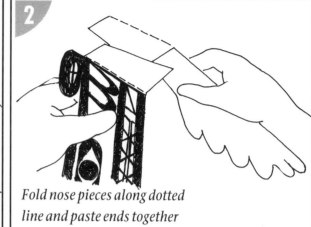

2. Fold nose pieces along dotted line and paste ends together

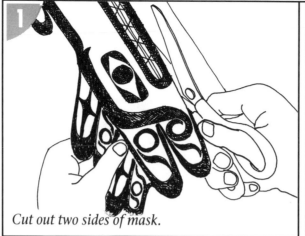

3. cut out 1" x 8" long head straps from tag board.

4. Paste head straps over the bridge of head.

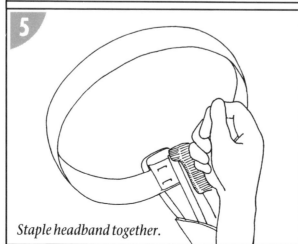

5. Staple headband together.

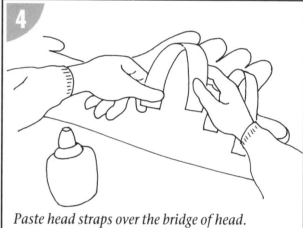
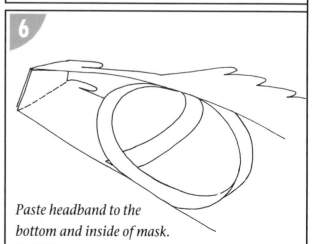

6. Paste headband to the bottom and inside of mask.

Adult Teaching Guide

The Cedar Plank Mask is the third book in a four part series, preceded by **The Bentwood Box** and **The Button Blanket**. This book is designed for students of 3rd through 6th grades, however, it can be used with younger students with modifications.

You may have used **The Button Blanket** or **The Bentwood Box**, in which case, you will recognize some similarities between the two dimensional art of the Northwest and of the style represented in this book. This style is called Westcoast art style by the people who live on the western most tip of Washington and the west coast of Vancouver Island (see shaded area on map). Because Westcoast style is an art form unto its own, there are differences between it and the northern styles. This book will help you see those differences in two dimensional or flat art.

You may wish to combine the activities of the preceding book with those of this book. In that case you should know that the Westcoast two-dimensional art is also painted on bentwood boxes, canvas or muslin to make robes and ceremonial screens. Because all other masks of the Nuu-chah-nulth, Makah and other Northwest Coast groups are sculptured, not flat, they follow their own special rules.

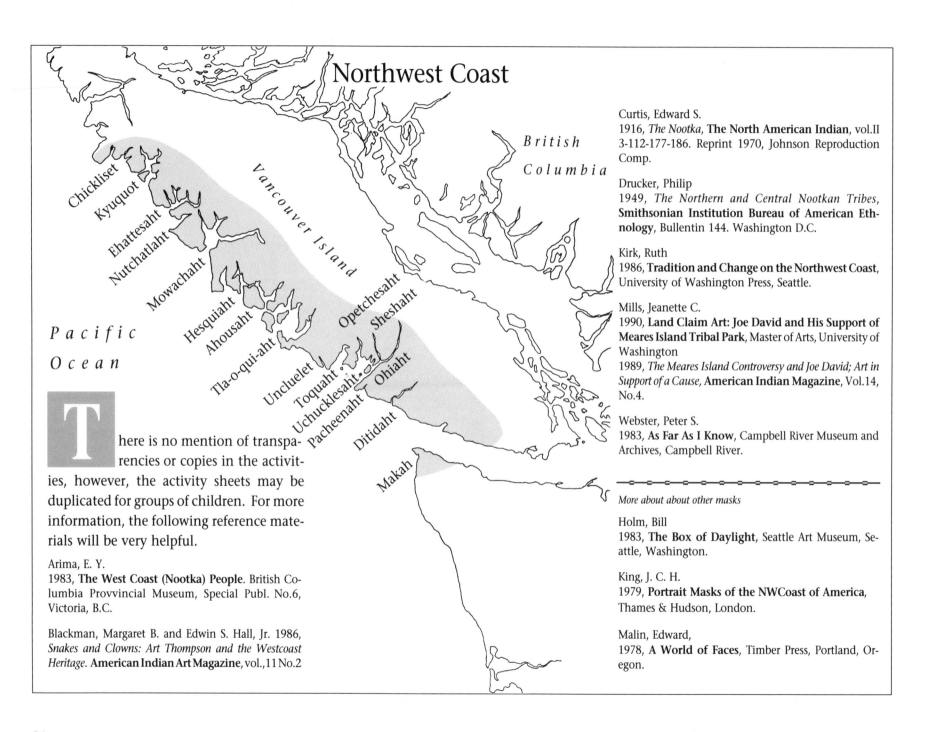

Northwest Coast

British Columbia

Chickliset
Kyuquot
Ehattesaht
Nutchatlaht
Mowachaht
Hesquiaht
Ahousaht
Tla-o-qui-aht
Uncluelet
Toquaht
Uchucklesaht
Pacheenaht
Ohiaht
Ditidaht
Makah
Opetchesaht
Sheshaht

Vancouver Island

Pacific Ocean

There is no mention of transparencies or copies in the activities, however, the activity sheets may be duplicated for groups of children. For more information, the following reference materials will be very helpful.

Arima, E. Y.
1983, **The West Coast (Nootka) People**. British Columbia Provvincial Museum, Special Publ. No.6, Victoria, B.C.

Blackman, Margaret B. and Edwin S. Hall, Jr. 1986, *Snakes and Clowns: Art Thompson and the Westcoast Heritage.* **American Indian Art Magazine**, vol.,11 No.2

Curtis, Edward S.
1916, *The Nootka*, **The North American Indian**, vol.II 3-112-177-186. Reprint 1970, Johnson Reproduction Comp.

Drucker, Philip
1949, *The Northern and Central Nootkan Tribes,* **Smithsonian Institution Bureau of American Ethnology**, Bullentin 144. Washington D.C.

Kirk, Ruth
1986, **Tradition and Change on the Northwest Coast**, University of Washington Press, Seattle.

Mills, Jeanette C.
1990, **Land Claim Art: Joe David and His Support of Meares Island Tribal Park**, Master of Arts, University of Washington
1989, *The Meares Island Controversy and Joe David; Art in Support of a Cause,* **American Indian Magazine**, Vol.14, No.4.

Webster, Peter S.
1983, **As Far As I Know**, Campbell River Museum and Archives, Campbell River.

More about about other masks

Holm, Bill
1983, **The Box of Daylight**, Seattle Art Museum, Seattle, Washington.

King, J. C. H.
1979, **Portrait Masks of the NWCoast of America**, Thames & Hudson, London.

Malin, Edward,
1978, **A World of Faces**, Timber Press, Portland, Oregon.

More about the story

Family

Michael lives with his grandpa and his mother. His mother isn't mentioned in the story but we see her in the first page. Michael might have brothers, sisters and a father. But, this story focuses on the special relationship which exists between Michael's grandpa and himself.

Family members, other than parents and siblings, living together is common among many groups of people, including Indian people. In the past, it was the norm for grandparents, aunts, uncles and cousins to live together as a family, an extended family.

There are advantages living in an extended family. Children have many people with whom they can share their sad and happy experiences. They learn to view the world in many ways. What about Michael? How might his life have been different if his grandpa had not lived with him?

Nuu-chah-nulth and Makah:

"Nootka" has for years been used as the collective name for the people who this name was derived from a mistake in communications between Captain James Cook and the Mowach'aht (see map).

These people lived in the inlet which Cook recorded as Nootka Sound. Today the Native term Nuu-chah-nulth ("All along the mountains") is gaining acceptance as the inclusive name referring to the people on the west coast of Vancouver Island. These people speak close related languages and have cultural similarities.

To the south, on the western most tip of Washington State, live the Makah. They share the same language and culture with their relatives to the north. The Makah people originally used the name of their village to identify themselves, but events of history changed this. In 1873 the United States Government demanded that parents send all children to a boarding school in Neah Bay. Eventually this action resulted in the families leaving their traditional villages. Makah has been used as the inclusive name ever since.

Using the map, have your children locate the different groups on larger maps of Washington and Vancouver Island. They will probably have fun saying the names. They will also appreciate why the artists themselves have given the name to their art, Westcoast art.

Masks:

Masks vary from one Northwest Coast Indian group to another. This variation reflects each group's as well as artist's style. Each carver starts with a basic shape common to his or her group, i.e. Westcoast style masks are made from planks and prism shaped blocks. As a carver continues carving, he or she follows special rules which indicate the form of the brow, eyes, nose, cheeks, mouth and chin.

The style of the mask will also depend on the character being represented, i.e. Kwakiutl Hoh-hok masks always have extraordinarily long beaks. Using the mask book list on the proceeding page have your students observe some of the masks' variations of mask types.

In 1884, the British Columbia government passed a law that made all "potlatching" illegal. This along with the reduction of the population by disease and the acceptance of Christianity, has led to the decline and even destruction of masks. It has only been in the last 20 years that a revival of mask making has surfaced.

The name "cedar plank mask" or "head

Color

dress" is a generic western name used to describe masks which are constructed from planks. Indian people do not refer to them in this way. They call the masks, both plank and sculpture, by the names of Lightning Serpent, Thunderbird, Raven, or Wolf. Each is important to an Indian family and its individual members. The right to wear one of these masks is a prerogative which is handed down from one generation to another.

For your own knowledge, you may want to read "The Wolf Ritual" in **The West Coast (Nootka) People** pgs.152-159, or "The Shamans' Dance" in **The Northern and Central Nootkan Tribes** pgs. 386-417.

An important element in the design of cedar plank masks is color. Black, blue (blue/green) and red are imaginatively applied, creating balance within the entire piece. This is most evident in the alternating colors of Lightning Serpent's feathers on the cover of this book. Notice, too, the treatment of color with the mouth, nose and eyes. Color is used to define each of the parts of head as well as shape. Once the children have colored their Raven (in Activity 1) they will be able to see how the colors alternate moving the viewer's eye from eye to nose to mouth and back again to the eye.

Traditionally, just as today, paints (pigments) were made from minerals. Northwest Coast Indians produced red from iron oxide, black from graphite, and white from lime. Blue paint from the northern part of the Northwest Coast, has been analyzed to be iron silica. All these minerals were mixed with oils, quite often salmon eggs, to make paint. Refer to **The Bentwood Box** for making paint with salmon eggs.

Group Activities

As an introduction, discuss with your children all the different kinds of masks they have seen and how they might be used. Most of the masks they will describe are full masks which cover the entire face and are sculptured. Discuss the functions of masks.

Using the books listed under "other masks" on page 26, show a variety of Northwest Coast masks. A field trip to a local museum might be planned. Introduce the idea of a mask being made from a flat plank by reading the story.

Activity I

1. Show the children the cover and through their observations, identify the Lightning Serpent, its head parts, and the colors which are used. (Tan is the color of the cedar wood.)
2. Hand out page 12 asking the children to color the Raven as indicated by the artist.
3. Discuss the differences and similarities in colors between the two.

Activity II

1. Hand out the Wolf designs on pages 13 and 15 to groups of children.
2. They should write down the head parts for each of the Wolves.
3. Hand out the Thunderbird design on pages 20 and 21 to each group.
4. Ask the children to study just the drawings to see if they can discover a totally different body part.
5. Help identify the claw or talons which appear on the Thunderbird design on page 21.

Activity III

1. Divide the children into groups of two children each.
2. Hand out pages 14 and 16, with each child receiving one Wolf design.
3. Help the children identify the thick black lines they are to cut along.

4. Hand out crayons (red, blue, and black) and scissors to each child to color. Cut out the parts and discard the gray pieces.
5. Have the children once again identify the head parts by matching with a partner as you call out different parts, i.e. nose.
6. Ask the children to put their pieces together again, like a puzzle.
7. Exchange puzzle parts and put the new puzzle together.

Activity IV

1. With the two different puzzles, have each group design a new animal by using the parts of both puzzles.
2. Ask each group to decide what design they would like to make, one of the original Wolves or their newly designed animal.
3. Hand out paste and construction paper for each group to make their own picture.
4. Share and discuss the pictures.

Westcoast Art Style

Earliest forms of Westcoast two-dimensional art can be seen in archeological materials from Ozette and among the early materials collected by Cook. Perhaps best known are two painted house-screens collected by Emmons which are now at the American Museum of Natural History. Photographs of these exist in the **West Coast (Nootka) People** page 170, **Art of the Northwest Coast Indians** by Inverarity, figures 10 and 11, and **Snake and Clowns** page 31.

These early art pieces capture early Westcoast art style as a mixture of geometric and free form design. These designs sometimes seem to represent internal body parts, sometimes external appendages, and sometimes magical powers. These special designs are both angular and loose, free forms. Geometric elements are also used along the borders of the pieces.

A prominent form which is used to depict the body parts, is the *"U" form.* It frequently depicts feathers and ears. The "U" form is readily seen in the art pieces within this book.

Group Activities:

In the following activities your children will learn some of the basic elements which predominate within Westcoast art style. These elements are some of the basic building blocks which your children will eventually be able to use to develop their own Westcoast art pieces.

Activity I

Preparation: With paper and pencil, trace around one of the "U" forms/feathers on the cover. Select one that shows bilateral symmetry so that you can fold it in half and both sides will be the same.

1. Show the "U" to the children, having them describe the form to you.
2. Ask them what it looks like. Ask them to speculate why in English it is called "U" form. (There is no trace of traditional names.)
3. Finally, fold the example in half displaying it's bilateral symmetry and ask the children to explain what has happened.
4. Introduce the term bilateral symmetry and ask for other examples.

Activity II

1. Hand out page 17 to the children.
2. Have them complete this page.
3. Then in small groups have them identify other "U" forms from pages 11, 12, 14 and the cover.
4. Individually with black crayons and paper, ask the children to draw some of their own "U" forms.
5. Finally, have the children examine the large ear of the Wolf on page 14 and the claw or talons on the Thunderbird on page 20. Speculate on the "U"ness of these designs.

Activity III

1. Hand out page 18 to the children.
2. Have them complete this page.
3. Ask them to identify these special designs on other art pieces in this and other books.
4. Have the students practice making these special designs.

Individual Style

As artists develop from apprentices to masters, their perceptions and techniques for delivering their own art matures. Each artist develops in his/her pieces elements which are like signatures. This is called the artist's style. Some artists' styles are so well known that their pieces are recognized without the artist signing his or her name to the pieces. This book presents two artists' styles within the Westcoast art style.

Through the evolutionary development of Westcoast art, a northern element began influencing some Westcoast artists. This element is Formline. If your children have studied **The Bentwood Box**, they will readily recognize this northern element. As it has grown to be part of many Westcoast artists' individual styles, the Formline has developed it's own West-coast flavor. It bends and curves through the paintings as though it has taken control of the paint brush itself. Then, with equal control, the Formline abruptly turns into a nearly geometric form. George David's art shows this influence as is seen on the Raven (page 12), the Wolf (page 15) and the Thunderbird (page 20).

Group Activities

YOU NEED

hand mirrors

enlarged copies of children's chosen mask designs on heavy weight paper (half as large).

Activity I

1. In groups of two have the children observe and record their observations of the Thunderbirds on pages 19 and 20.
2. Then in larger groups have the children discuss their findings. Each child can take a turn being the spokesperson.
3. As a total class, search in the book for the other art pieces by each artist.

Activity II

1. Each child may select a favorite mask design from the book. (Note: You may want to enlarge these so that they fit on the children's heads in the customary fashion.)

2. Hand out mirrors to each of the children. (If you do not have enough mirrors, some children can "eyeball" it.)
3. Ask them to place the mirror at the edge of their sheet. (Allow time for exploration!) Discuss and define the term "mirror image".
4. Now ask the children to place the mirror at the front of the Thunderbird's beak. Allow the children to take a good look at what is in the mirror.
5. With paper and pencil have the children draw a mirror image of their design.

Activity III

Using pages 22 and 23, and the needed materials, have the children complete their masks.

Activity IV

If your children would like to make the Lightning Serpent Mask, use page 24 and copies of the cover which are available (see order form at the end of the book).

The Northwest Coast Indian Art Activity Books

Nan McNutt

This series of fun activity books features the art and culture of Native Americans from Northwest Coastal areas—including the Tlingit, Haida, Tsimshian, Bella Bella, Kwakiutl, and Salish. Each book is reviewed for cultural accuracy by tribal members and uses the work of Northwest Native artists. Activities are field-tested in classrooms, and each volume provides an Adult Teaching Guide. Ages 6-10.

Also of interest—A great resource for Northwest Native culture and travel!

Native Peoples of the Northwest: A Traveler's Guide to Land, Art, & Culture
Jan Halliday and Gail Chehak
In cooperation with the Affiliated Tribes of Northwest Indians

SASQUATCH BOOKS
SEATTLE

Nan McNutt
& Associates

Available at bookstores or order from Sasquatch Books, below:

The Bentwood Box, ISBN 1-57061-116-5, 36 pp, $10.95   qty _____ $ _____

The Button Blanket, ISBN 1-57061-118-1, 44 pp, $10.95   _____   _____

The Cedar Plank Mask, ISBN 1-57061-117-3, 36 pp, $10.95   _____   _____

The Spindle Whorl, ISBN 1-57061-115-7, 44pp, $10.95   _____   _____

Native Peoples of the Northwest, ISBN 1-57061-056-8, 256 pp, $16.95   _____   _____

Subtotal   _____   _____

Tax (WA residents only; add 8.6%)   _____

Shipping ($4 for first book, $1 for each additional)   _____

TOTAL   _____

SHIP TO: Name_____   Address _____

City_____   State _____ Zip_____   Phone_____

☐ Check/Money Order enclosed   ☐ Visa   ☐ Mastercard   Account #_____   Exp date _____

Signature _____   Printed name _____   Phone _____

Send order to: Sasquatch Books, 615 Second Ave., Ste. 260, Seattle, WA 98104   (206) 467-4300; Fax (206) 467-4301; Email: books@sasquatchbooks.com

Or call TOLL-FREE: (800) 775-0817 — Ask for a free catalog of all our Northwest, children's, and Native American titles!